ANGER MANAGⴰⴰⴰ
KIDS WITH ANGER ISSUES

The Practical Solutions To Emotional Outburst, Short Temper, Impatience, Stress, Anxiety And, Depression In Children

COPYRIGHT

DEDICATION

I specially dedicate this book to all children worldwide including my dearest daughter.

TABLE OF CONTENTS

CHAPTER ONE

BASIC INTRODUCTION TO ANGER ISSUES

As a parent or guardian, it is normal you
have to deal with an angry child. Most
times, we end up in an intense shouting
match with our kids, or we become so
confused about the next thing to do
when an angry outburst happens.

Anger is typically a normal emotion in kids and adult depending on how it is expressed; it is normal if it's constructive while it's terrible if it's destructive. It is experienced by everyone, no matter how gentle they seem to be. No one can claim he hasn't got angry before. It usually occurs in children as a result of unpleasant feelings they experienced when they think they have been mistreated, injured, opposed in opinions and other clogs in the wheel of attaining their personal goals.

From a young age, we were told not to be angry or appear sad, but these only results in repressed feelings. While it is necessary sometimes to suppress our anger to avoid physical confrontations like fighting, but suppressing these anger always might lead to severe health and mental problems like anxiety, depression, high blood pressure, digestive and sleeping issues. It can also lead to passive-aggressive behaviors that hinder an interpersonal relationship with others.

As a human, we get angry sometimes to maintain the equilibrium between our feelings, so, when we feel the fear, hurt, pain, disappointment, grief is too much, we tend to burst out our rage. Though the anger doesn't necessarily stop the hurt, but we feel emotionally balanced and temporarily numb the pain, that's how humans fight any perceived threats by attacking it.

Anger in children, if left unchecked can leads to aggression (which is destructive), defiance, temper tantrums, disrespect and other problematic issues if your child doesn't know how to deal with his/her emotions. Not only this, aggression in the childhood days such as fighting, teasing, spitting, and bullying etc. can result in academic problems, narcissism, peer rejections and poor mental health in adulthood.

So by teaching our kids how to identify and deal with anger, we are actually preventing it's adverse effects before they happen. Children need not be aggressive but assertive to be able to express themselves without getting too emotional or defensive.

CHAPTER TWO

WHY IS YOUR CHILD SO ANGRY?

Anger is also known as "the fighting emotions"; it is a secondary emotion. Your child feels an emotion first, which is the primary emotion; after this, he/she feels displays the secondary, which is "ANGER". As an observant parent, you need to study yourself and see what is happening around or what you are doing to bring out the rage in your child.

The primary emotion is the one you need to learn and discover as soon as you notice any emotional changes. Below are the most common triggers of primary emotions before transitioning to anger:

FRUSTRATION: These are issues that occur when the child is tired of something affecting him or her personally without much help from anyone, these can come in the form of lack of knowledge, low self-esteem, fear of mistakes, communication problems amongst other factors.

BIOLOGICAL ISSUES: These are issues that directly affect the child personally, which includes tiredness, coping with hormonal changes during puberty, hunger, and so on.

STRESS AND ANXIETY: These are issues that can also bring out the anger in children, they include; sickness, home relocation, looming divorce, a new teacher at school, struggling with upcoming exam or tests in school, and so on.

THREATS TO SELF-ESTEEM: These are serious issues that need to be taken seriously because you can't compare the emotion of children to that of the adults. You need to get into action immediately as soon as you notice any of these signs;

Inconsistency in the enforcement of rules

The feelings that a particular sibling is more preferred to him or her.

An open correction that resulted in embarrassment and public humiliation

Low empathy for others

Being bullied

Lack of sense of autonomy

Seeing family members arguing and being angry with one another

Witnessing injustices done to others

Being misunderstood and his or her opinions rejected

Friendship problems

If you can identify and solve the
following problems in your child, he or
she will not need constant battle with
anger again. But sometimes it might not
be evident to you or child while he or she
is angry; in this case, it is essential to
work out a way to identify such a
problem.

NOTICEABLE BODY SIGNS OF ANGER IN YOUR CHILD

Intense clench in the teeth

Tense in the muscles

Clenching of the fists

Stomach churns

Faster heartbeat rate

CHAPTER THREE

THE EXTREME WARNING SIGNS: HOW TO SPOT THE SIGNS OF EXTREME ANGER IN YOUR CHILD

Spotting the signs of anger early in your child is very important and can help your child in making positive decisions on how to handle anger issues. Observe and talk about what your child feels when he or she is angry. Below are some of the potential warning signs of anger you should seriously take into consideration:

1. Using Aggression To Have His or Her Way: Aggression should typically be the last action to take after a wave of anger, but kids with anger problem often use aggression as their first attack in defense.

2. Your Child's Emotional Rage Is Destroying Interpersonal Relationships: Though it's normal to be angry once in a while, and it's normal to hit siblings or call names once in a while. But if your child own is too much, and he or she is getting angry at any little thing, this will definitely affect him later in life in developing a healthy relationship with others if proper action is not taken against it as soon as possible. No one wants to be with someone who gets angry all the time, and it's pissed off kind of attitude.

3. YOUR CHILD'S BEHAVIOR IS KILLING YOUR FAMILY LIFE: It is a big negative sign if you notice your child is disrupting your daily activities and your family life. Not being able to attend some family events or succumbing to your child's will are just some temporary solutions to anger issues that will result in serious problems later if left untamed. If this is continually happening to you, families and friends might dissociate themselves from you, because it's definitely going to affect you emotionally, as you won't have much time for yourself.

4. STILL DISPLAYING TEMPER TANTRUMS WHEN HE OR SHE IS AGED ENOUGH: As a child grows older, he or she tends to drop some habits. However, if your child's temper tantrums continue to get worse as he or she becomes older, then there's a severe problem that shows he or she is finding it difficult to regulate his or her emotions. It's normal for a 3 year old kid to throw him or her self on the floor and kick his or her feet when he or she is angry, but that's so weird and abnormal for an 8 year old child to do so. At this stage, training and coaching are vital to correct this issue.

5. YOUR CHILD HAS NO SHOCK ABSORBER FOR FRUSTRATIONS: As kids mature, they tend to develop more tolerance for frustrations and anger. For

example, if your 8 year old child destroys a toy game just because he or she didn't win or shreds his or her books because of an ink stain on it, this shows that your child is suffering from serious anger problem.

UNDERSTANDING THE ANGER PROCESS IN YOUR CHILD AND HOW TO USE EMOTIONAL REGULATION STRATEGIES EFFECTIVELY

Anger, just like any other problems, needs to be understood because it requires different processes before it builds up to what it is. Below are the outlines you need to master for better understanding and possible solutions to the anger your kid is exhibiting:

Situation Selection: This is a process that involves choosing to avoid or ignore some situations according to their likely emotional effect.

Situation Modification: This is a process that involves the efforts to modify a situation to change its emotional impact.

Attentional Deployment: This is a strategy that involves channeling or diverting one's attention towards or away from an emotional situation.

Cognitive Change: This involves adjusting how one appraises a situation to alter its interpretation or emotional meaning

Response Modulation: This is a process that involves doing some things to modify the experiential, physiological, or behavioral aspects of an emotional response.

The above emotional regulations can be applied according to how the situation comes, using the above method has proved effective, try it, it works.

CHAPTER FOUR

HOW TO EFFECTIVELY MANAGE THE ANGER ISSUES OF YOUR CHILD

Pay Attention To Your Emotional Reaction When He Or She Is Angry:

It is so important to lead by example, and this is the way to go about it. You have to pay attention to both your physical and mental reactions when your child is angry. You will definitely know when someone is upset when they are in your presence, and you will feel your heart rate beating more faster because your

adrenaline rush is so high at that
moment.

Though it's not easy to calm down in
such a situation, but you need to calm
down to teach your child how to handle
his emotions when he or she is also in
the presence of someone angry. If you
didn't calm or respond harshly, trust me,
this is how he or she is going to be

behaving with you and others too.

Remember the saying; "Two wrongs

can't make a right."

Provide Consequences For Bad

Behaviors And Not The Anger

The moment your child gets angry,

screams and throws tantrums around

and seems to have lost his or her cool,

give him the consequences for his

behavior and no for his emotions

because anger is a normal emotion, kids

also get angry the way we adults do.

However, if he uses foul language,

swears at you during his emotional

outburst, in this case, you must give him

the consequences for his or her usage of

those foul language and curse words. If

his or her anger is not breaking any rules

and doest turn to disrespecting you as a

parent, you should allow them the

chance to be angry — children just need a

safe space to let the steam off, and they will come back to normal afterwards.

Don't Yell At Or Challenge Your Kid When He Or She Is Angry

Most parents often deal with an angry child by yelling and challenging their kids. Though it's not easy to implement but doing this will make you lose your control. The appropriate thing to do at this moment is to keep calm at the heat of the rage.

Constant yelling or challenging will just equip him or her with more energy and grow into resentment, which might be so difficult to control later, it's like adding more gas to fire. If you remain calm, the tension will definitely come down, he or she will be relaxed and will be the one to apologize later, which this you win.

Don't Reason Like Your Child When He Or She Is In Enraged

It is so awkward to reason alongside with your child when he or she is angry, an adult will always be an adult, and the capacity to contain situations as an adult is totally different from how a kid will contain it. So it's better to leave that verbal space for him or her, keep talking to a minimum, make sure you use a clam, neutral and quiet tone.

Phrases you can say at that moment are:

> *"I love you."*
>
> *"I want to help you."*
>
> *"I am here for you."*
>
> *"Let me know when you are ready."*
>
> *"I understand how you are feeling"*

Create A Calm And Safe Spot For Your Child

Some kids are aggressive in their anger when they are hurt; they sometimes destroy things around them, throw books, shred books, and so on. If this applies to your child, it will be helping you create a safe and calm spot where he or she can go to when angry. In that safe spot, make sure you remove every item that might be thrown at or can cause injury out of there. It will also make sense if you can make his or her room a safe spot too by removing any items that may cause harm, with time and with this approach he or she will learn to control the anger issues.

Don't Allow Your Emotions To Be Used As A Bait

Some parents become overwhelmed and freeze up when their kids throw tantrums or screams at them, which makes them paralyzed with indecision and gives in to the child using them as a bait.

If care is no taken, your child will take advantage of you by getting angry intentionally to engage you. Your child might bait you by doing something terrible or saying something rude because they know you will give in, reject the bait, don't get angry and don't give in. If you give in, you are teaching the child that it's cool to act that way. Instead, let him calm down and lecture him or her on how to use his or her problem-solving skills.

Don't Give Too Harsh Punishments

It is not good enough to give your child harsh punishments at the heat of anger; it will only make you lose your proposition. Doing this will only strengthen him and see nothing special in punishment because he or she has grown a thick skin for it. The more you escalate the punishment, the more he or she keeps doing the worst things, that is

why it is necessary to control your

emotions in order not to lose your grip.

Though it might be hard to implement,

remember the goal is to teach your child

how to have good emotional control, you

can't lose your emotional control and

expect your child to have it, he or she is definitely learning from you how to handle situations.

Don't Get Physical With Your Kid

It is terrible to get physical with your child, as explained earlier, you shouldn't go into your child's role. You are a role model to him or her and its important to be a good role model. Remember if you are getting physical with your child, you are just teaching him aggressive ways to solve problems. Though it's annoying to overlook some things but there are other methods to deal with a mouthy or rude child rather than getting physical with him or her. Instead find a way of expressing his or her feelings with you, making recommendations for methods he or she can understand.

Encourage Or Reward His Or Her Improvements

Like everyone else, we love to be praised or encouraged; this is also applicable to children too. You discourage a child who gets angry right? You also need to encourage a child who has changed in his or her emotional outbursts, make him or her feel good, look for his or her strengths and share your appreciation for this change and possible reward him or her. By giving him or her accolades when the right changes are effected, it will definitely push him or her to improve more.

Keep A Log Book Of Activities

Write out a log of activities and events that results in the emotional rages and how it was finally resolved, don't write only what your child did wrong but also include what you and others did wrong too. As you continue in making changes, you will want to know how things are improving, though the blow-ups can't just vanish overnight but take some couple of time. Don't give up.

Don't Send Him Or Her Away To Calm Down On His Or Her Own

It is a wrong idea to let a child go figure out his or her anger issues alone, your aim when your child is angry is to calm her nerves down and restore in him or her a sense of safety. Instead of giving him or her a time out to figure all the scary, big feelings alone, it is better to help in moving through his or her feelings, and you will be amazed at how he or she begins to get more emotional control as he or she feel connected and not alone.

Help Your Child Develop Emotional Intelligence

It's so unfortunate that most kids don't feel comfortable emotionally in expressing their uncomfortable feelings. Most times, some of these kids are sent away, thereby discounting their fears; they never received any help needed to handle their emotional discomfort. They tried hard to repress their feelings and concerns, but these later results in pain, fear and grief which make kids angry unnecessarily. So it is necessary to keep an open arm to your kid and allow him or her to express any of his or her discomforts freely with you, this makes him or her develop good emotional intelligence.

Quick Ways To Help Children Express Their Anger

Pop bubble wrap

Write a letter to someone

Rip paper

Do wall push-ups

Jump on a trampoline

Talk about it

Scribble on a paper and squeeze it

Do jumping jacks

Do stretches

Wrap your hands around yourself and
squeeze

Squeeze a stress ball

Put the palms of your hands together
and release it later

Squish playdough

Write down what's on your mind and rip
it off

CHAPTER FIVE

CHILDREN'S ANGER LEVEL INDICATOR TEST/QUIZ

The test below is intended to show the various level of anger exhibited by your child. Children practically indicate one or more of these signs. Still, if your child shows most of these signs consistently, then there should be a serious concern. Okay, let's go down to the test.

Below is a rating according to the appropriate scale you can classify it into, please make sure you are truthful and sincere to yourself to get the best results, the ball is now in your court. Let's go!

Kindly rate each statement according to the scale provided between 1 to 5, and make sure you place your ratings in the right place.

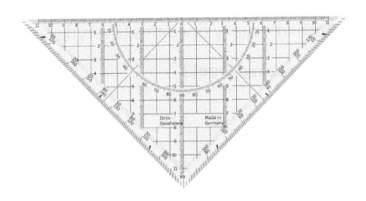

CHILDREN'S ANGER SCALE

1. My child hasn't done this or rarely does

2. My child does this once in a while (Not more than once monthly)

3. My child often does this (Once or more in a week)

4 My child usually does this (Everyday or Many days in a week)

CHILDREN'S ANGER SPACE

_____1. My child blamed others for his or her problems

_____2. My child throws and destroys things whenever he or she is frustrated or irritated.

_____3. Anytime my child is angry, calming him or her down requires a lot of appeasing

_____4. My child doesn't want any change at all, and when a change is forced, he or she gets angry

_____5. My child changes the rules of games anytime he or she is playing with other children

_____6. My child utter hateful or spiteful things whenever he or she is stopped

_____7. My child intentionally slows down and reject instructions on what he or she is supposed to do, this makes discipline a standoff for him or her

_____8. My child looks for arguments or reasons to become upset, even when everything is at peace

_____9. My child rebuke, reject and complains about others

_____10. My child loses control whenever he or she is angry, and she displays her via body language and facial expressions

_____11. My child uses bad language whenever he or she is angry

_____12. Whenever my child is learning new things, he or she gets fed up easily and wishes to do another thing.

_____13. My child is stubborn and does not do what he or she is supposed to do unless you speak in the right tone or cool approach.

_____14. My child friends don't like to play with him or her because of aggression.

_____15. My child easily fights with other children and find it difficult controlling his or her emotions when teased

CHILDREN'S ANGER TEST RESULTS

1 – 5: Your child is not prone to frustration and free from anger issues; it's cool but don't change him or her from this.

6 – 10: This is an average degree of anger and irritation. A level of nearer to 10 is

normal for younger children (Like Age 5 or below) and a level lesser than 6 is more appropriate for older children.

11 – 15: This indicates that your child is gradually attaining an above-average degree of anger. A much score is still appropriate for younger kids, but at this junction, you have to sit tight and be vigilant.

16 – 20: This shows your child has an anger issue and urgent attention needs to be given at this point.

20 and above: This shows your child has a severe anger problem that needs

urgent attention, immediate steps to cope with his anger needs to be taken to help him or her cope with the problem.

HAPPY READING

OTHER BOOKS BY THE AUTHOR

You can also get this book written by me (Bella Stardom) which emphasizes on how to teach children in respecting their personal space and those of others.

It is available in both Kindle and Paperback, kindly check the image or the links below to grab a copy.

Kindle:

https://www.amazon.com/dp/B07ZZ95R17

Paperback:

https://www.amazon.com/dp/1705462871

CONTACT THE AUTHOR

For any enquiries, suggestions, feedbacks
and any other information; you can
contact the author by email at
bjstardom06@gmail.com